COUNTRYSIDE
NEEDLECRAFT SOURCE BOOK

COUNTRYSIDE
NEEDLECRAFT SOURCE BOOK

LYNETTE MOSTAGHIMI

ANAYA PUBLISHERS LTD
LONDON

First published in Great Britain in 1992
by Anaya Publishers Ltd, Strode House
44–50 Osnaburgh Street
London NW1 3ND

Editor: Patsy North
Designer: Sheila Volpe
Special photography: Di Lewis
Artwork: Tony Bellue, Michael Volpe, Julie Ward, Kate Simunek

British Library Cataloguing in Publication Data
Mostaghimi, Lynette
Countryside: Embroidery sourcebook.
I. Title
746.44

ISBN 1–85470–090–1

Typeset by Servis Filmsetting Ltd, Manchester
Colour reproduction by J. Film Process, Singapore
Printed and bound in Singapore by Times Offset Ltd

CONTENTS

INTRODUCTION

Images of the countryside lend themselves beautifully to being translated with needle and thread into embroidery and have provided inspiration for decorative textiles throughout the centuries. Flowers, hedgerow plants, trees, birds, animals and insects have all found their way on to large-scale lavish historical embroideries as well as embellishing humbler, more utilitarian items around the home.

Natural images like these still have just as much appeal today – perhaps particularly so for town-dwellers who can bring something of the countryside into their homes through their embroideries. Plants and animal life can be observed all around us on a country walk, and it is great fun and very rewarding to record some of our favourites in a sketch book or with a camera to build up as a reference for future embroidery designs.

In this book, I aim to fire your interest and imagination by showing a wide range of beautiful embroideries inspired by the countryside, from practical decorative stitchery to 'fine art' pieces. The fascinating differences between them lie in their interpretation – in their composition and in the colours, textures and stitches chosen. I have also designed a stimulating selection of trace-off motifs which you can combine and interpret as you please.

This is a book to dip into if you want to find a particular motif on a countryside theme – perhaps a meadow flower or a farm animal – but it is also a book to help you to develop your own ideas by combining the various elements in your own way. Remember, too, that there are many methods of working the same motif – in free-style embroidery, in needlepoint or cross stitch, in appliqué or quilting. Choosing from the wealth of ideas which follow, you can make the decisions about colour, type of thread, size and arrangement of motifs to create your own individual work.

For beginners, I have provided plenty of straightforward patterns in the form of tracings and charts to start off with. But for the more experienced embroiderer, there are wonderful inspirational pieces to show the endless variety of ways in which countryside themes can be portrayed. Some include fabric painting and machine stitchery, which are often used by designers to add depth and interest to their work.

Others are worked entirely by hand, sometimes combined with applied materials such as net, organza or leather for texture and special effects. With these ideas, I hope to encourage you to experiment with your embroidery stitches and techniques, so that you can produce more original, personal and satisfying results.

OPPOSITE This magnificent panel is called 'A Day in the Country' and shows how successfully countryside themes can be interpreted in embroidery.

Chapter 1

HEDGEROWS

Tangled, mysterious and teeming with life, hedgerows are an inexhaustible source of pleasure, renewed seasonally with the changing colours of blossoms, fruits and flowers. Hazel catkins and pussy willow in the spring, dog roses in the summer, hips and berries later in the year and interesting foliage and wildlife all year round — these and many other natural delights await you on country walks.

9

PREVIOUS PAGE *This intricate three-dimensional panel is worked entirely by hand, using an imaginative selection of yarns and fabrics for realistic colours and textures.*

As well as a great variety of plant life, an abundance of animals, birds and insects make their homes in the cover of the hedgerows. The smallest of details in amongst the intertwined branches can catch your eye and draw you into a miniature world, ready to be transformed with needle and thread into beautiful embroidery designs.

On country walks, I usually fill my pockets with fallen leaves, unusual pieces of bark, stones and the occasional flower, all of which are preserved on my return home and arranged in a special book with pages of plastic pockets. The tiniest objects are tucked into the pockets and form an instant resource of natural colour and pattern. I add my ideas and developments too, building up the character of every page with colour-matched threads, fabric swatches and drawings.

RIGHT *Some of the delights of the hedgerow are brought to life in silky threads on this black satin evening bag. The stitching is very fine and delicate.*

OPPOSITE *The dog rose on this pot pourri sachet suggests the evocative scent of summer flowers. Perfumed sachets are quick to embroider and always make charming gifts.*

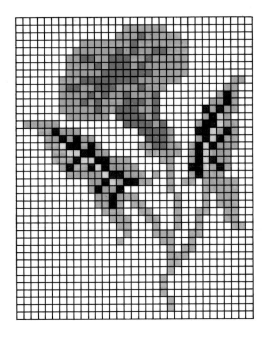

BELOW *This convolvulus flower is depicted in delicate silk stitching on satin lingerie for a very luxurious look. It is worked in cross stitch over waste canvas.*

I enjoy interpreting the textures of natural objects into stitches, and hedgerows are full of contrasts here. There are rough gnarled branches, smooth shiny berries, lacy cow parsley, fluffy old man's beard and frilly-edged hawthorn leaves to name just a few. I make use of the full range of embroidery threads available to convey different surfaces, from wools and matt soft embroidery cottons to shiny pearl cottons and real silk yarn.

The fabrics on which I stitch play an important part in my embroideries too. For a natural-looking background I might choose calico or an unbleached linen, while for vibrant colour and a touch of luxury, silk and satin are wonderful to work with.

You can use the trace patterns on pages 14–19 freely to develop your own unique work. Choose a natural palette of colours for subtle harmony or, for a dramatic effect, try working a design in black on white. Alternatively, white thread on a fine white fabric gives a delicate traditional look.

LEFT *Ivy finds its way into most hedgerows. The leaf has a strong simple shape which is combined here with wayside blossom on a needlepoint glasses case. Gold beads sparkle at the flower centres.*

OPPOSITE *The same ivy leaf design is used on a needlecase as a single bold motif.*

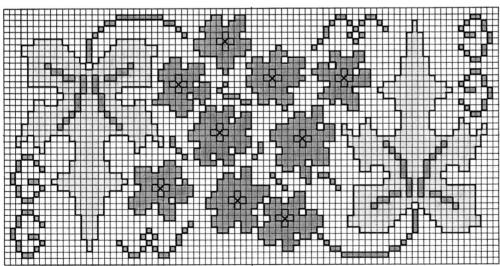

The corner design on this page could be worked in buttonhole stitch on the collar of a fine linen blouse or on a small tablecloth or mats. The honeysuckle motif opposite is ideal for delicate clothing, embroidered, quilted or appliquéd on to silk and sprinkled with pearl beads. You can add colour to a child's dungarees with a border of acorns, slipping in an occasional padded ladybird or snail for humorous effect.

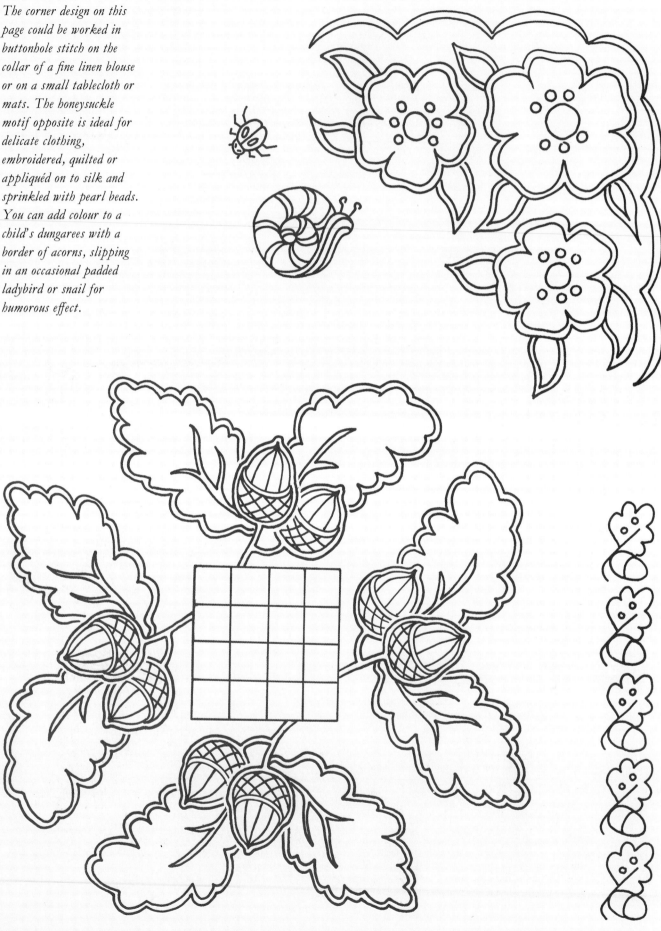

This selection of motifs has a wintery feel with holly and ivy designs. Use the motifs to decorate festive tablecloths and napkins for special family occasions. You could experiment with the ivy border in appliqué, or even stencil the leaves with fabric paint and then work embroidery stitches for the veins, tendrils and tiny berries.

The floral designs opposite can brighten up a range of items and would particularly suit pillowcases, blanket tops and valance frills. Squirrels, robins, acorns and flowers on the border of a corduroy skirt could be coordinated with a single squirrel motif embroidered on to a sweater for a complete country-style outfit for a child.

BUTTERFLIES

Butterflies have been a favourite theme for embroidery through the centuries and this is hardly surprising, as few other creatures display such a diversity of colour and pattern as they do. They often appear in Chinese embroideries, worked in the finest of stitches in glowing silken threads, and were also popular motifs in samplers and crewel work. To me, butterflies are synonymous with beauty and life, and conjure up memories of hot shimmering summer days.

PREVIOUS PAGE This shows part of a superb carpet embroidered in wool. The glorious colours of the butterflies are achieved by blending the yarns and 'painting' with the needle.

The beauty of butterflies and their value as inspiration to the embroiderer lie in the balance and proportion of colours and the fascinating arrangements of patterns in their wings. The shaped wing edges, too, translate effectively into border designs for embroidered articles, repeated and reversed as you wish.

I first used butterflies as a design resource at college, where I picked out borders and used the wing 'eyes' in some examples and the abstract pat-terns in others to create a collection of decorative gloves. Having discovered the astounding variety of colours and shapes contained in these little forms, I return again and again to gather ideas from butterfly books and museum collections.

You can work butterflies in needle-point or free embroidery, but for a life-like appearance, I like to use shiny threads like stranded cotton and pearl cotton. For really special projects, silk threads look spectacular.

Stranded cotton brings a sheen to the wings of these orange tip butterflies. Embroidered in cross stitch on linen, they make a charming composition with flowers and grasses.

This bold butterfly motif is worked on stiff plastic canvas to make a tissue box. The wing patterns, although not so detailed when interpreted in wool, make an interesting design, easy for a beginner.

The butterfly is a beautiful motif for both garments and household linens, worked individually or in a group. A cloud of butterflies would look wonderful fluttering over a roller blind for a special window covering. Bright colours are especially suitable for these designs but they would look equally effective in white thread on a white background. For a three-dimensional effect, embroider your butterfly on to felt, then cut it out and apply as if it has just landed.

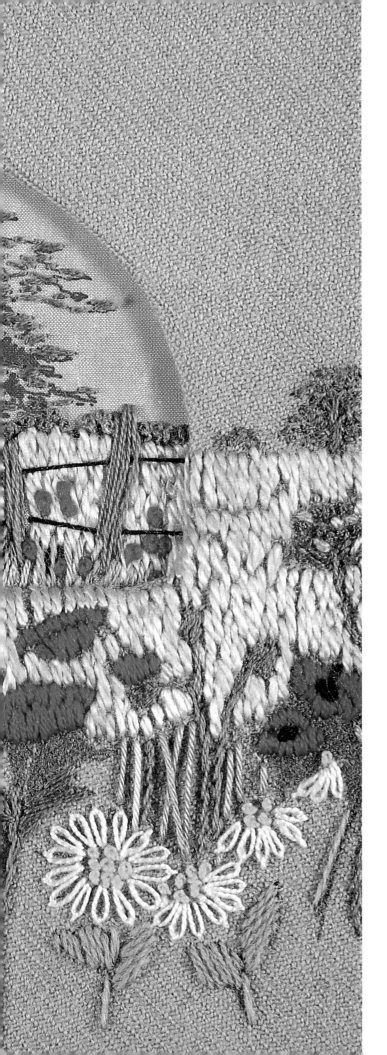

Chapter 3

FLOWERS OF THE FIELD

The flowers of the field are the wild uncultivated blooms which somehow manage to slip through the farmer's crops to burst into colour against all the odds. From a distance they are like tiny embroidered details on a patchwork quilt of fields. They are often daintier than garden flowers, with small flower heads and delicate petals. But some, like the poppy or the thistle, are more imposing and make brilliant splashes of colour against the ripening crops.

PREVIOUS PAGE Poppies and daisies worked in free-style embroidery draw the eye into this country scene.

A colourful selection of flowers that you might see on a country walk are combined on these cushions.

Wild flower forms have a simple harmony of their own and readily adapt to embroidery and appliqué. Field poppies were particular favourites during the Art Nouveau period, appearing in opulent full bloom on a host of decorative articles.

I find that meadow flowers combine well into the prettiest of intertwined borders with trailing leaves and ribbons. I also love a sprig muslin effect with tiny blooms in pastel colours scattered over a light fabric. During the nineteenth century, christening dresses were often decorated with designs of this kind, worked with great skill in white thread on white fabric. Hours of stitching went into these garments which eventually became treasured family heirlooms.

Field flowers with their trailing stems decorate this unusual clutch purse. They are worked in cross stitch on hessian, but, for a daintier effect, could be embroidered in shiny threads on a finer fabric.

Flower designs embroidered on to garments give them style and individuality and are quick to do. A tiny sprig of flowers or a thistle embroidered on to a canvas shoe, a jeans pocket, a beret or a pair of gloves give a distinctive personal touch. Those most familiar of field flowers, buttercups and daisies, are especially suitable for children's clothes, evoking images of carefree days playing in the meadows.

One of my favourite ways to use wild flower motifs is to work them in fine embroidery and then mount them in a frame or as a card for a thoughtful gift. Decorated pot pourri sachets are always well-received too. For something larger, scale up a design, thread a bodkin needle with thick wool and scatter meadow flowers over a blanket or sofa throw in bright colours for maximum impact.

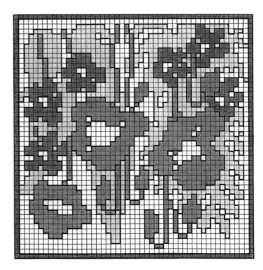

The poppy and the violet make a richly coloured pair for this little needlepoint pincushion for your own work basket or for a gift. This one has a dark background, but you could choose a light colour for a summery look.

Stylized meadow flowers are gathered into a loose bunch for an informal cushion design. They are worked in detached chain and straight stitch, and French knots. Wool, soft embroidery cotton or even narrow satin or tubular ribbon can be used for a bold effect.

31

With these designs you can add a personal touch to a whole variety of articles. For example, embroider silky flowers along a buttonhole band, repeat a row of clover along the hem of a skirt, or scatter sprigs over a duvet cover. Be creative with your stitches to add texture and interest. Try bullion knots or beads for flower centres and seeds, or mohair yarn for the dandelion and thistles.

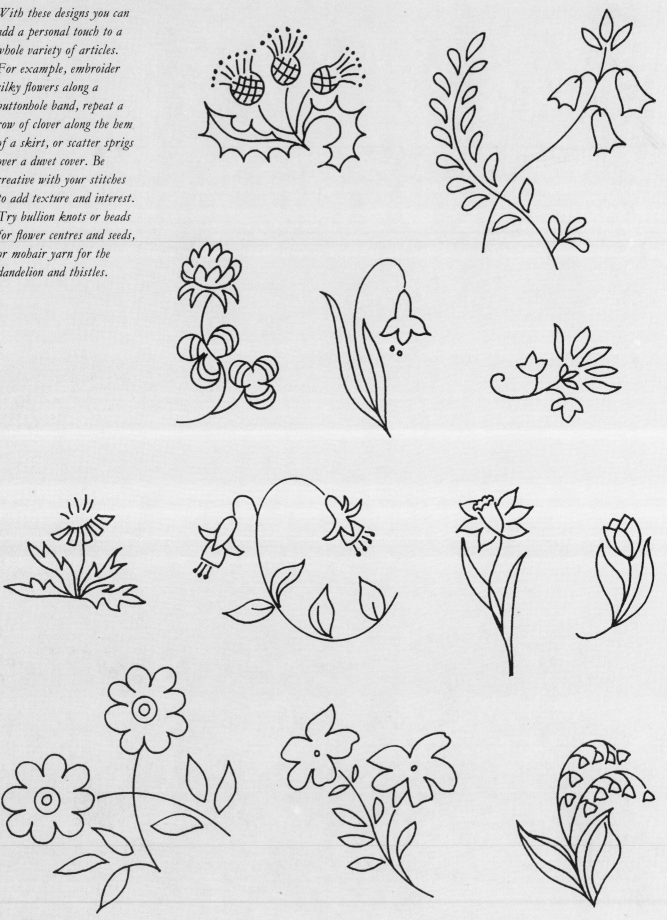

In the style of traditional crewel work, these motifs could be embroidered on to cushions, using muted tones for a faded 'antique' look. Alternatively, for brightness, choose sharp colours that jump to the foreground. Subtle three-dimensional effects can be achieved by padding areas lightly with felt, then working the embroidery over the top.

This selection of borders would look beautiful along the edge of tablecloths and napkins for a country look. For a special touch to a bathroom towel, work the embroidery on a satin ribbon, then appliqué this to the towel. In addition, you could pick out an individual motif to embroider on to other table or bathroom linens to give a coordinated look to the collection.

Chapter 4

WIND AND WEATHER

The wind and the weather of the colder seasons of the year add dynamic qualities of movement and drama to scenes of country life and conjure up all kinds of images far-removed from the sultry days of summer. When I walk in the countryside at these times, I still find plenty to fuel my imagination in the shapes of the clouds, the falling leaves, the snow softening the contours of the landscape or the wind-swept skyline. With less colour in the surrounding scene, this can be an opportunity to explore rather more muted thread combinations.

PREVIOUS PAGE The trees on the winter landscape were worked in machine embroidery on vanishing muslin and applied to the painted silk background. The grasses, fence and other details are worked by hand.

RIGHT Fine machine and hand embroidery stitches on a painted silk background suggest the delicacy of wind-blown seeds in this exquisite miniature picture.

Imagine clouds scudding across a stormy sky, glinting raindrops slanting across a barren landscape or bare trees against a snowy field. These images would make unusual monochrome pictures and suggest the use of metallic threads and silvery beads. But there are colourful motifs to be gleaned from windy days too. One of these – a traditional scarecrow dancing in a field – is a rare sight today, but one fondly remembered from childhood stories. This motif would suit casual country wear for youngsters, embroidered on to a dungarees bib in stranded cottons or on a sweater in wools.

Another motif synonymous with a windy day is the kite. This is always associated with bright colours and the simple shape, like the example on page 43, is easy for beginners to work. Why not add a real tail to your embroidered kite, made from a length of cord and tied with ribbon bows.

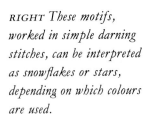

RIGHT These motifs, worked in simple darning stitches, can be interpreted as snowflakes or stars, depending on which colours are used.

OPPOSITE Fallen leaves turn the woodland path into a mass of rich russets, oranges and golds. The scene is softened with layers of net and the main features are worked in free surface embroidery.

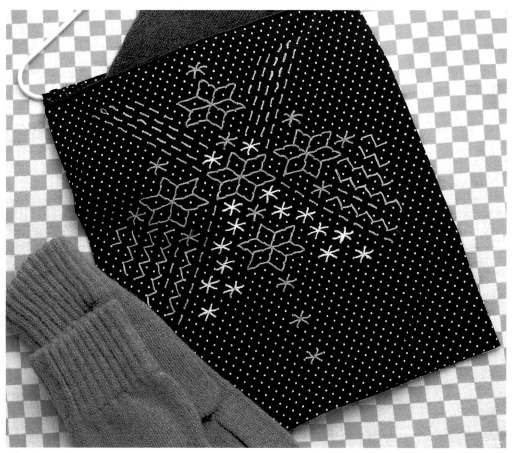

This witty rainbow cushion is made in appliqué using shiny fabrics. Here the motifs have been stitched down with machine zigzag stitch, but you could just as easily use buttonhole stitch or slipstitching.

Splashes of raindrops or the dispersal of downy seeds can be explored for delicate effects in embroidery, using a single strand of thread or pearl beads – perhaps to embellish evening wear or lingerie. On the other hand, I would envisage the sun or a rainbow being worked in more solid stitchery, couching or appliqué while quilting would be perfect for fluffy clouds.

Other motifs which represent the weather to me include snowflakes and snowmen. There are endless design possibilities in a single snowflake, which would look appropriate on a winter scarf or cap, or worked in metallic thread on an evening bag. For a splash of colour in the midst of a winter scene, you could embroider a simple dressed-up snowman or a Christmas tree ablaze with lights for a very special Christmas card in cross stitch or free-style embroidery.

The kite motif is easy to work in cross stitch. Using waste canvas, you can embroider it on to denim or cotton to personalize children's clothes.

This collection of motifs represents windy, showery weather and would suit outdoor garments such as jackets, waistcoats, hats, scarves, gloves and jeans. The umbrella border would brighten up plain hems, cuffs or braces, with a few raindrops worked in pearl beads for a touch of sparkle. Vary the direction of satin stitches to create a variety of tone as the light is reflected in different directions.

There is something for winter or summer among these motifs. For a coordinated look in the nursery, you could embroider or quilt clouds on to cot linen and add matching appliqué motifs to the curtains. The snowflakes would give a stunning evening look, scattered over a black top. Work them in metallic thread with beads or pearls, concentrating the design at the neckline.

46

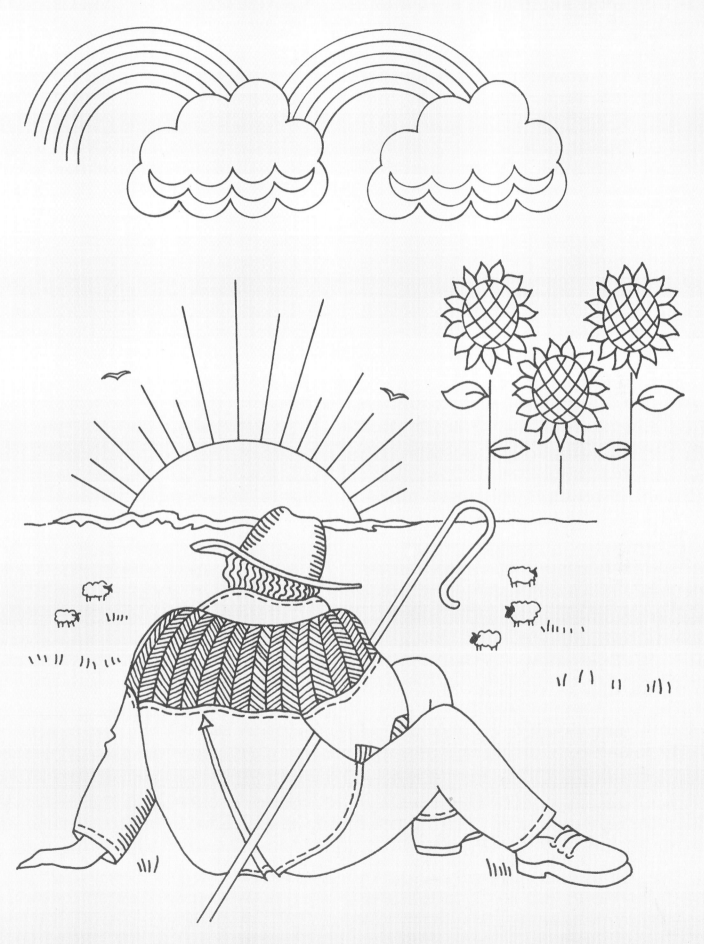

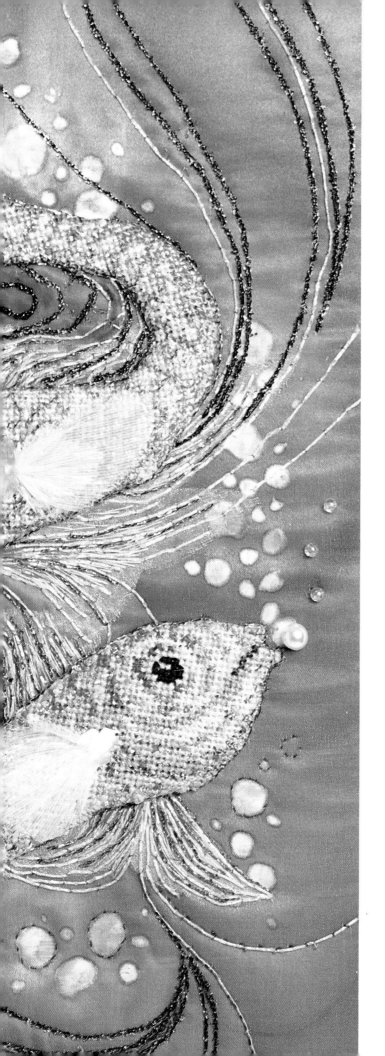

Chapter 5

WATERLIFE

Water always attracts activity and interest. Just sit for a while beside a pond, stream or river and soon you will see the surface bubbling with life. Somehow this busy environment manages to have a calming effect on the onlooker with its slower pace and gentle rhythm. And what better way to spend a peaceful interlude by the water than with a sketch book to record some of the plants and wildlife?

PREVIOUS PAGE *The effect of light glinting on water and on the fishes' scales is achieved with metallic thread, opalescent fabric and pearl beads. The fish are worked in needlepoint and applied to the painted background.*

The brilliant plumage of the kingfisher diving down to the water is portrayed in richly coloured woollen yarns on a beautiful needlepoint panel. It is worked in tent stitch to bring out the detail of the bird's feathers and the weeping willow leaves.

The flowers of the water-lily and the flag blossom in country ponds. Theirs is a classical beauty with style and elegance, which translates well into quilt and appliqué designs. For colour, work these motifs in subtle tones of shiny embroidery threads, using long satin stitches which reflect the light, then add a dragonfly or two, worked in metallic gold or silver for extra sparkle.

These little creatures are fascinating in their colouring and movement. The dragonfly motifs on page 56 were based on those I saw skimming the lily pads at home in Brighton, in a nearby rock garden. They were unusually plain with the exception of a bright turquoise tip to their tails.

This impressive water-lily panel in fact uses a very simple technique, ideal for beginners at embroidery. It is worked in long satin stitch on canvas. Each petal is well-defined and the background shows the ripples on the water.

The glint of light on the darting body of a dragonfly is achieved by using shiny threads on this exquisite little jewellery box. Here it is worked in cross stitch on plastic canvas, but it would also make an ornamental motif for a jacket lapel.

Many of the creatures which inhabit the water or the banks of ponds and streams make wonderful subjects for embroidery. Fishes and frogs have marvellous profiles with great potential for creative design and pattern development. Their shapes suggest movement and liveliness which can be interpreted by the use of bright, lively colours. Fishes' scales are full of rainbow hues which can be enhanced by mixing together different shaded strands of cotton in one needle for a shimmering effect.

Ducks and ducklings are much loved by children and translate well into cross stitch for motifs which can be used on clothing or in the nursery. Swans have a similar appeal, singly or in pairs.

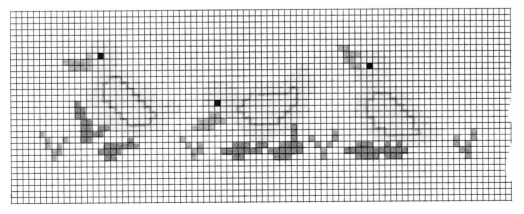

Ducks waddling along in a row are bound to appeal to children and are a perfect design for the nursery. The ducks are worked in cross stitch on evenweave fabric which is attached to the pillowcase with bands of satin ribbon.

Fishes are always fun to work in embroidery or needlepoint. There is plenty of scope for imagination in filling each patterned section with your own stitch variations. Beads, sequins and metallic yarns really complement this theme, as they have the reflective qualities associated with water. The newt could look quite stunning couched in gold thread and beaded, imitating a brooch for an evening dress or jacket.

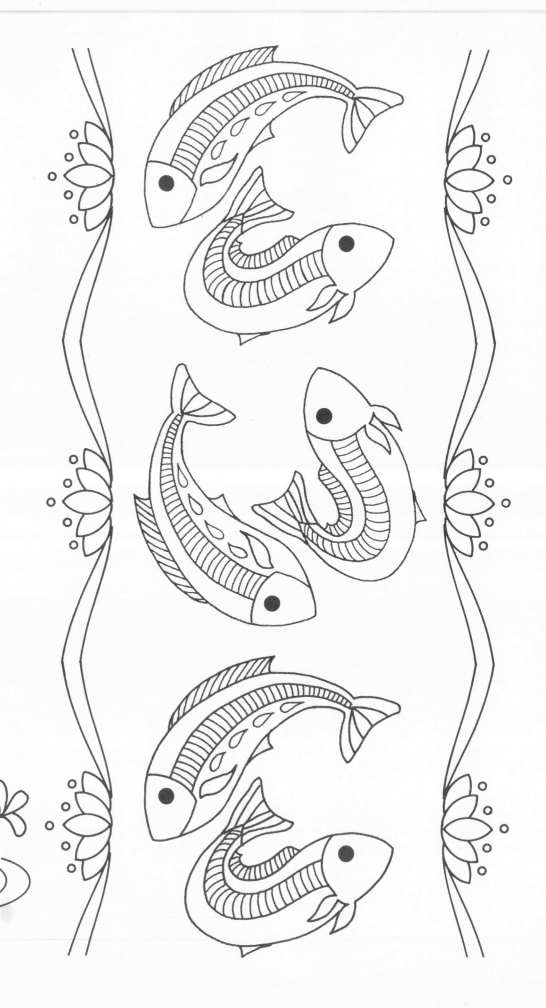

The water-lily and dragonflies shown on this page would look wonderful at the corner of a tablecloth and on matching napkins. If you add a touch of gold thread to the flower centres and dragonfly wings, this will 'lift' the design from the fabric. The pond and riverside birds make attractive motifs on bathroom linens and curtains. And why not use your motifs in a different way – painted or stencilled on to walls or furniture for a coordinated look.

For a scene from a country childhood, trace the picture of the children fishing and transfer it to fabric. You can then combine embroidery techniques with fabric painting. Paint soft skin tones and blend turquoise blues and greens for watery effects. The dyes will add a softer dimension to your work to contrast with the embroidery threads. You could stitch the birds on to a painted 'watery' background in the same way.

Chapter 6

BIRDS

As a child growing up on the edge of the countryside, I loved attracting birds into our garden, especially the more unusual varieties which I would eagerly rush to identify in an encyclopedia. Today, I continue to be fascinated by the charming variety of the species and find that they make ideal subjects for embroidery of all kinds, translating well into needlepoint, cross stitch or free-style embroidery. Realistically portrayed in their natural habitat or used as a stylized design motif, birds have universal appeal.

When I am researching for embroidery ideas, I sometimes make use of the resources available at the British Museum in London or at my local Booth Museum in Brighton, where there are specialist books and wonderful collections of stuffed birds.

I look specifically for colours, patterns and textures, then experiment with a simplified version or perhaps concentrate on colour proportions to create geometric arrangements. It is an approach which can yield some interesting ideas and spark off new designs. For example, I spent some time studying the actual structure of a bird's wing and tail, and this led to the development of a garment which opened to reveal coloured embroidery carefully positioned between pleats and folds.

Mother Goose and her goslings make a colourful needlepoint picture for a country-style interior. Animal families always appeal to children, too, so this would make a delightful gift for a nursery.

Bird motifs are always charming and adapt to all kinds of articles. These designs have a rather stylized decorative quality. The larger motifs would look stunning worked on to a lampshade, or in borders on curtains and blinds. The scalloped border would look very appealing on a baby's cot or pram quilt.

The owls on this page have been simplified to make them suitable for appliqué and quilting as well as free-style embroidery. Younger children could work the little owls in colourful oddments of felt with added stitching to make bookmarks, simple gifts and cards. The thrushes shown opposite would brighten up a kitchen, worked with brilliant red berries and glossy leaves on to a tea-cosy and tray-cloth.

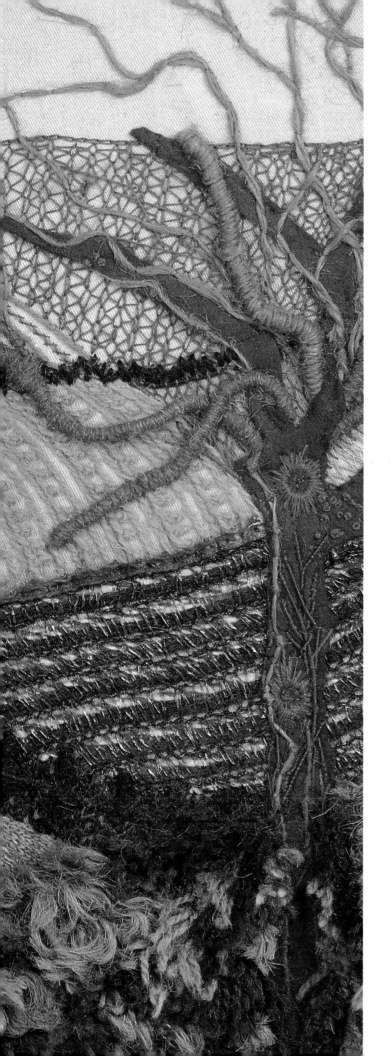

Chapter 7

FARMS

Farming scenes make interesting embroidery compositions by portraying rural activities and environments. There are examples of historical embroideries which give us a glimpse into the lives of agricultural workers of the time, showing their costumes, tools and livestock. Many images spring to mind when I think about farms, from the farmer himself, at work on the land, to the cultivated landscape around the farm buildings. There are the familiar animals, too, always popular with embroiderers.

PREVIOUS PAGE
Interesting textures are achieved in these hand-embroidered fields by using a wide variety of stitches and woollen yarns of different thicknesses. The farm cottages are worked in appliqué, some of it slightly padded.

OPPOSITE *This idyllic farmyard scene is embroidered in a variety of shiny and woollen threads to emphasize the different textures of the hens, the gate and the fields.*

RIGHT *Worked in close, fine hand stitches, the sheep in this exquisite little panel are full of character and have a silky texture.*

Images of 'The Farmer's Lot' are appealing, although often seen through rose-tinted glasses with man working in harmony with nature. Throughout the centuries the fine arts and decorative arts have recorded this romantic partnership and I continue this tradition with some of the trace patterns which follow.

The idea of the farmer at work could be developed into a needlepoint picture, bringing in other elements of the environment like the ploughed fields, the ripe crops or animals, domestic or wild. There is great scope for rich colours and textures here, with the use of different yarns and needlepoint stitches.

Farm buildings, too, make good subjects for embroidery, whether you prefer to work a realistic representation of a farm you know, or indulge in a dream cottage, thatched and whitewashed, with roses round the door.

Children love farms, especially the animals. I always feel there is an element of fun associated with farm animals, probably due to our familiarity with their looks and characters. In years gone by, fables and folk tales exaggerated and embellished animals' habits and exploits; today it is cartoons and videos generating popularity.

Some of the motifs on the following pages could be enlarged on a grid or on a photocopier to a size which would make them suitable for 'toy' cushions for children's rooms, perhaps in appliqué with embroidered details. You could explore the fun element with a child's quilted 'farm' jacket with additional, lightly padded animals, separate from the jacket but attached to the surface with Velcro or tied into the nearest pocket with cord.

For a light-hearted touch in your sitting room, make a series of 'sheep' cushions for a sofa and count them as they leap from one cushion to the next along the row.

A dream farm cottage with a rambling rose and a vegetable garden. This little picture is easy to work in cross stitch with details in back stitch and French knots.

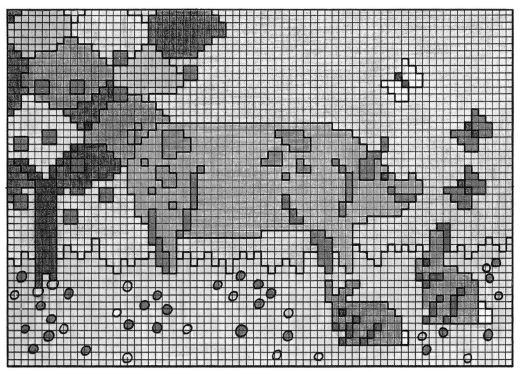

This naïve needlepoint picture would look delightful in a country kitchen or child's room. French knots are added for the flowers and fruit.

These farmyard scenes add a humorous touch, and could be enlarged and worked in counted thread or free-style embroidery for fun cushions, bags and wall panels. For children, use toy eyes on the animals for a life-like effect, but make sure they are firmly fixed to the fabric.

Smaller farm images are always appealing worked in bright colours to add interest to plain linens or children's clothes. You could range the foxes, mice or hens along the edge of tablecloths, nursery curtains or skirt hems. And the sheep would look enchanting bounding along on a pyjama jacket or dressing gown.

Chapter 8

HARVEST

Fields golden with the ripening crops, red and green apples hanging heavily on their boughs, succulent berries dotting the hedgerows – harvest is a colourful and happy time, and to many people a time of reward for hard work throughout the year. Orchards, fields, woods and market gardens are all full of inspiration for embroiderers during this season, with nature's offerings coming to fruition and images of the harvest everywhere.

PREVIOUS PAGE *Layers of coloured net form the background to this detail of a field at harvest time. The textured effect of the grasses and flowers in the foreground is achieved by innovative use of surface embroidery stitches.*

RIGHT *A field of ripening wheat is depicted with great subtlety in a beautiful panel inspired by some lines of poetry. It is worked by machine in silk on a silk background.*

The word 'harvest' conjures up for me memories of hot sunny days, bright luscious fruits and the gathering together of produce for harvest festivals. There is an abundance of ideas for embroidery at this time of the year, and it is a chance to use rich glowing threads to represent the ripe crops.

It is a good time to go out with a sketch book or a camera to record the shapes and colours of the fruits and vegetables in their natural setting before they are picked, to observe close-up the difference between the various cereal crops and to capture the effect of the fields from a distance, as they form a variegated patchwork of yellows and greens.

Gathering in the hedgerow harvest is always a special treat, especially as the bounty is free. Blackberries and elderberries make attractive motifs, with pretty leaves to set them off, and would make wonderful trailing borders.

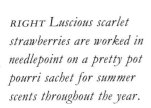

RIGHT *Luscious scarlet strawberries are worked in needlepoint on a pretty pot pourri sachet for summer scents throughout the year.*

OPPOSITE *Raspberries make an unusual decorative motif for this linen clutch bag. The fruit and border dots are worked in close satin stitches for a slightly raised effect, while the stems are in stem stitch.*

Bunches of plump grapes in rich purple enhance the deep reddish-brown of the mahogany box lid. The grapes motif would also suit cross stitch work on table linen.

One of my favourite designs using harvest fare is celebrated in the Evesham pattern of Royal Worcester porcelain, in which blackberries, apples and pears combine with cob-nuts, corn-on-the-cob and asparagus to form a beautiful composition. The fruits of the harvest illustrated on the following pages can be similarly combined into a lavish design or used individually. They need colour and a touch of imagination to really bring them out.

Beads are perfect to represent blackberries and raspberries, and shiny threads will accentuate the gleam on the skin of ripe fruits. A mound of fruit in a bowl or bunches of grapes make very successful quilting designs, while apples, pears and plums are simple shapes to work in appliqué.

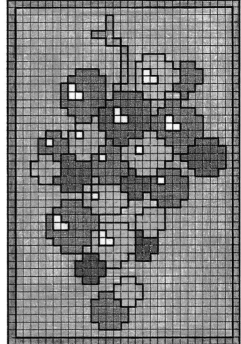

Ripe fruit harvested from the orchard makes an appropriate picture for the kitchen. The needlepoint is mounted by lacing it over stiff board.

For borders and single motifs, pick ideas from these two pages and let your imagination run riot with the colours. The fruit can be appliquéd on to a tablecloth at random or used to decorate summer clothes. The shapes can be outlined very simply with back stitch or filled in with long-and-short stitch, satin stitch or chain stitch following the contours of the fruit. French knots are perfect to build up blackberries and raspberries.

The charming figures of the boy and girl on this page are just asking to be embroidered and mounted in a frame. You can combine appliqué and stitching with fabric painting, bringing in beadwork for the cherries. Think of kitchen linens such as tablecloths, napkins, curtains, oven gloves and aprons for the other harvest motifs, perhaps coordinating a whole set of items.

The circular designs shown opposite suit table mats and round tablecloths or cushions, teamed up with a border of berries. The diamond motifs could be dotted about within the patches of a patchwork quilt, and are the right shape to embroider between a diagonal cable pattern on an Aran sweater to add detail and interest.

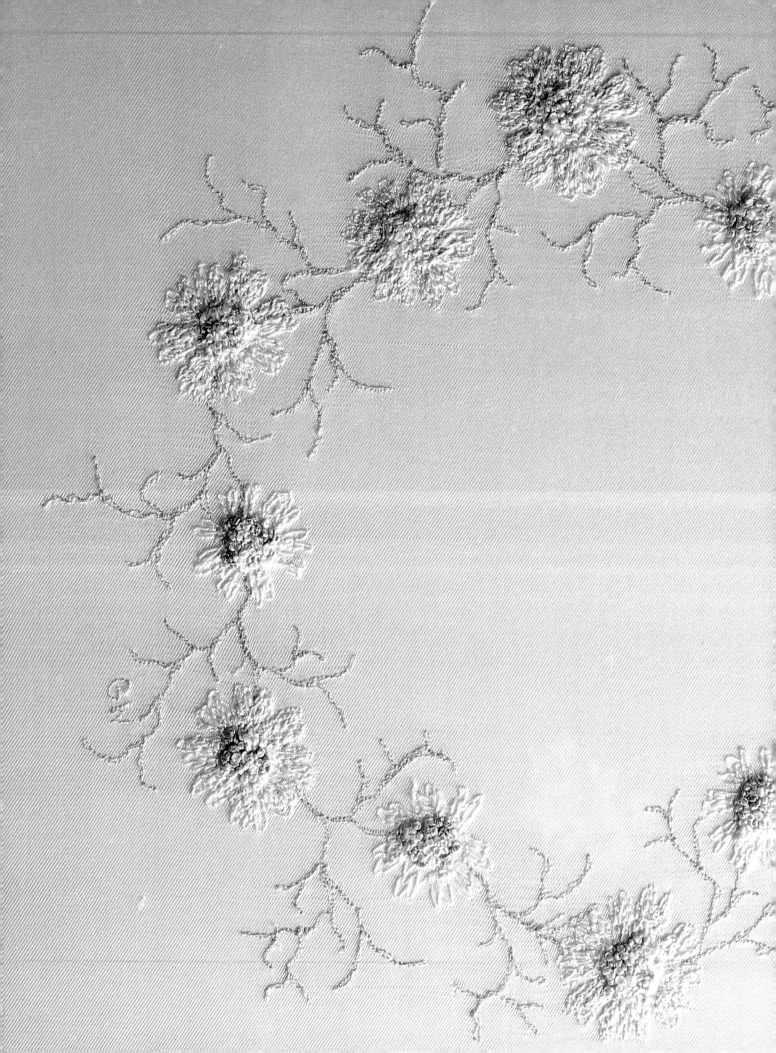

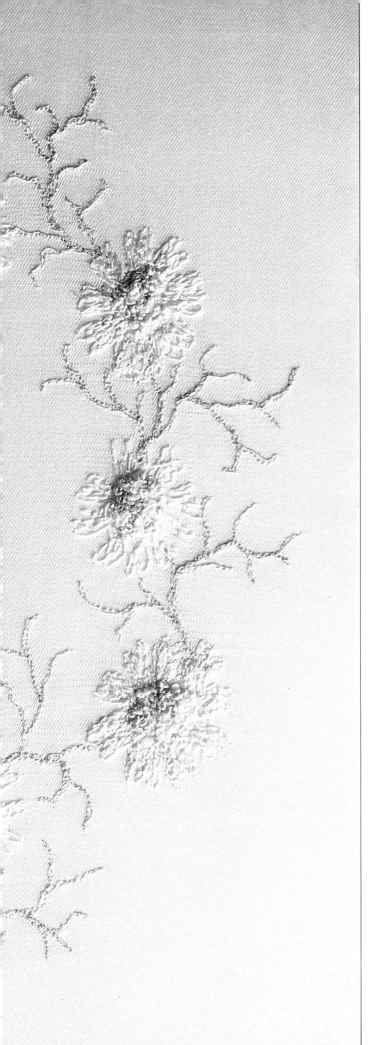

Chapter 9

GARLANDS

The circle on which the garland is based has been used from early times to symbolize many things — love, friendship and re-birth among them. The beauty of a garland in embroidery lies in the balance and harmony of the design with its circular or semi-circular framework. Garlands can be composed of numerous different elements. Leaves and flowers can be combined with fruit, berries or ribbons for a lavish arrangement, while a simple garland can be made up of basic leaf shapes, almost with a stencilled effect.

Inspiration for garland designs can come from a whole range of sources. I often look at the natural garland shape of the borders around china plates for ideas, especially some of the beautiful old-fashioned floral designs. Other ideas might come from magazine illustrations, painted mirror frames or, the most obvious resource, the florist's garlands.

For the best effects, balance large patterns with small ones, strong colours with weaker ones. To achieve complete harmony in a piece, choose colours in equal proportions of light, mid and dark tones. These need not all be in the same colour range; mixed colours with varied tones will have the same effect. To check that colours work together, simply arrange the embroidery skeins in three piles of light, mid and dark tones and you will soon see the strengths and weaknesses of your chosen threads.

RIGHT *These dainty flower garlands are worked in satin stitch, stem stitch and bullion knots on fine broderie Anglaise pot pourri sachets.*

OPPOSITE *Leaves of different shapes in light and dark shades of green are twisted into garlands on a set of needlepoint cushions. They form effective frames to the wild flowers at the centre.*

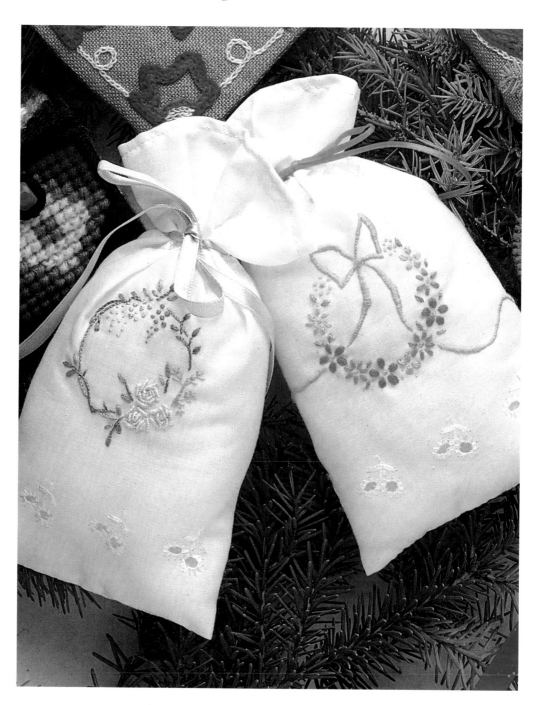

There is a hint of the turning season in this garland of leaves and bright berries which forms the centrepiece of a small tablecloth. Satin and back stitches are used for the embroidery.

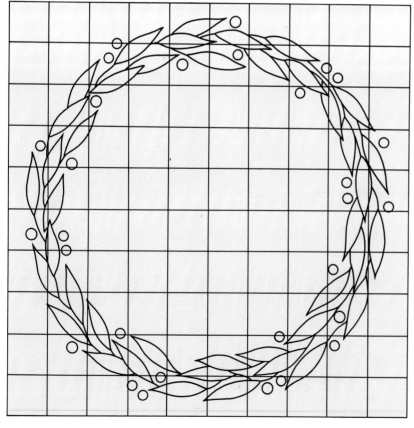

A garland of flowers or berries makes a natural centrepiece for a round table-cloth, but would also work well on a bag, a cushion, a patch pocket or simply as a picture. Garlands can create areas of interest scattered over a large, plain item such as a duvet cover.

For more versatility, leaves and flowers can also be arranged as swags for borders to be used on table and bed linen or around the edge of a curtain. The selection of country garlands and swags on the following pages have seasonal overtones with fruits, flowers and wildlife appropriate to various times of the year. It would be a nice idea to display your embroidery to suit the season. Use the spring flower garland on a cloth to set off a vase of daffodils, perhaps, or make a festive cloth for Christmas with a wreath of holly, ivy and mistletoe leaves in shiny threads on a richly coloured background.

This delightfully old-fashioned garland emphasizes the delicate fabric of this broderie Anglaise pouch for tights or stockings. The flowers and ribbon are simple to embroider in satin stitch and detached chain stitch.

Each garland on the opposite page is based on a circle of seasonal fruit or flowers with some wildlife added too. Worked in a variety of stitches with areas of texture provided by French knots or glass beads, they would make beautiful embroidered pictures, framed in a brass fitting. For a larger, more ambitious project, work the May Day dance in bright fresh colours in needlepoint or free-style embroidery.

Both garlands and swags are illustrated here. The swags could be embroidered along the scalloped hem of a tablecloth or curtain, combining them with fabric painting for an unusual effect. They would also make a beautiful decoration for a padded fabric photograph frame for a special picture. The enclosed circle on the right could be the basis of a cutwork design for a small linen tablecloth.

Chapter 10

WOODLAND

Walks in the peace of the woods bring you closer to nature and develop an awareness of our wonderful heritage of flora and fauna. As twigs snap and leaves rustle underfoot, attention is drawn downwards to the forest floor and, with every season, a feast of colour, form and pattern is revealed to inspire the embroiderer. Look up instead and there are intricate patterns of twigs and branches against the sky. Deciduous woods and pine woods each have their own atmosphere and are full of rewards for the keen-eyed.

PREVIOUS PAGE Dyed fabric, scraps of organza, net, metal threads and strips of leather are combined with machine embroidery to give an impression of leaf litter on the forest floor.

ABOVE RIGHT The delicately coloured embroidery of aspen trees is worked on a painted background in satin, stem and straight stitch with some couching.

I find all kinds of things to inspire me on a woodland walk and often gather a few fallen leaves, seeds, cones or nuts for my collection of natural objects. I also like to make bark rubbings, as these can reveal surprising patterns to interpret into stitchery. The play of light through the tree branches is endlessly fascinating, too, and you can capture the atmosphere with a camera and use the photographs as reference for future ideas.

The bluebell season must be one of the prettiest times of the year in the woods, just waiting to be portrayed in stitches. But each season brings its delights, with a treasure of surprises in store from the fabulous forms of fungi to bright lichens, berries, ferns and the turning leaves.

RIGHT This interpretation of bluebell woods is worked in wool, cotton and rayon threads, and also torn strips of fabric. The scale of the stitches gradually diminishes to give a sense of perspective.

OPPOSITE The contrast between dark and light areas makes this machine-embroidered panel a dramatic portrayal of a woodland scene in winter.

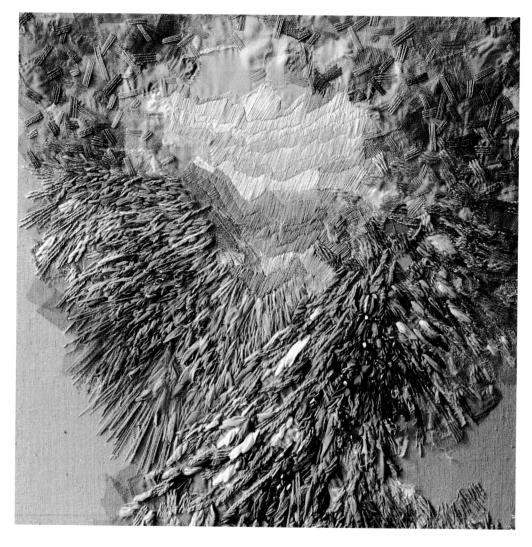

A woodland glade, filled with colour and dappled light, is the subject of this evocative panel detail which combines silk painting and stitchery.

Heather often blooms at the edge of woods and makes a wonderful embroidery motif. Here heather plants make a feature of a curtain tie-back.

Although there is only dappled light, some beautiful plants grow in the woods. Some, like fern fronds, lend themselves well to embroidery, and bluebells, primroses, snowdrops and violets add a splash of colour.

If you are very quiet and patient, and very lucky, you may see the woodland animals and birds. Some, like the woodpecker, have distinctive patterns which would make dramatic embroidery designs in satin stitch or cross stitch. The fallow deer, on the other hand, is camouflaged to allow it to blend into the background. This elegant creature has a beautiful dappled coat which could be worked in soft whites and warm tans on a natural fabric. To give a spark of life, add a tiny bead or pearl to the eyes of birds or animals to represent reflected light.

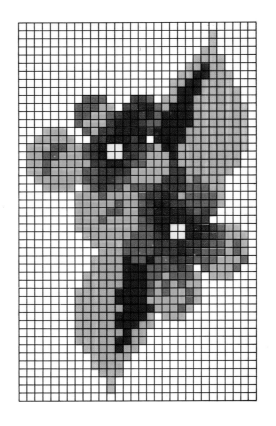

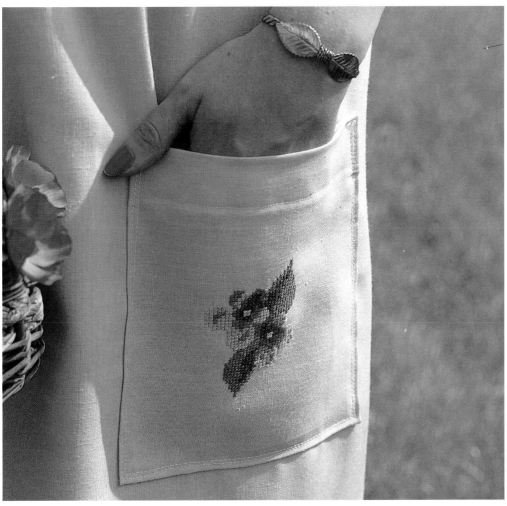

The violet has a timeless appeal and makes a charming decoration for a pocket, a blouse, a bag and many other items. This motif was embroidered in cross stitch over waste canvas.

This selection of woodland plants and animals can be used for all kinds of items. The little owls can be worked in wool to give a fluffy quality to the rows of blanket stitch or interpreted in layers of frayed felt, built up from the feet to the head. Details such as toy safety eyes would really add to this design for children. The deer can be realistically embroidered in long-and-short stitch, picking out the deep bright eyes in black metallic thread.

The traditional-style panel would make an unusual centrepiece for a crewel work cushion cover. For something big and more spectacular, try enlarging the pattern in sections on a photocopier to a size that would fit a fire-screen or even a chair back. An embroidered chair cover is an ambitious project, but stunning results could be achieved relatively quickly with thick wool and a bodkin needle. Several of the other designs shown, such as the toadstools, violets, seeds and leaves, can be worked as borders or as individual motifs.

Chapter 11

GARDENS

Gardens are a constant source of inspiration to me and I often spend an hour or two sketching in friends' gardens or in the grounds of country houses near the South Coast where I live. At any time of the year, gardens provide a wealth of ideas for embroidery, whether you prefer to focus on the fine detail of petal and leaf shapes or take in a broader view of the colours, outlines and textures of flower beds, shrubberies and paths. Each season brings new delights which I can add to my sketch book and interpret into stitch patterns.

I am fascinated by the variety of flower forms, from the opulence of a full-blown rose to the delicacy of the tiny plants in a rock garden I often visit in Brighton. The strong graphic quality of a gladioli stem, for example, would conjure up a completely different style of embroidery from a scattering of forget-me-not flowers. Again, I might use a tulip – a simple regular shape – as a motif for an embroidery in a modern setting, whereas the curving petals of the columbine or the dainty flowers of honeysuckle would suggest to me a charming old-fashioned design to be worked in soft colours.

Leaf shapes, too, are worth recording – feathery, strap-like, heart-shaped, spiky or serrated – like petals, the variety is astonishing. Leaves make wonderful borders and corner motifs, alone or with flower heads.

RIGHT *That rather formal flower, the tulip, is interpreted here as a stylized design which would fit in with a modern or a country setting.*

OPPOSITE *The regular pattern on this summery floral cushion is built up from a rose motif worked in colourful cross stitch on evenweave fabric.*

A full-blown rose and a bud are set off to perfection by the dark background on this needlepoint pin cushion. A border of black lace would give the pin cushion a more ornate, Victorian look.

The garden flower motifs I design often lend themselves to a variety of embroidery techniques, and different interpretations of the same idea can result in surprisingly different effects. Worked in free embroidery, flowers can be as fresh and realistic as those in your garden, while translated into a counted thread technique such as needlepoint, they can look bold and geometric or charmingly naïve.

While on the theme of gardens, don't forget the vegetable garden, which is such a delight throughout the seasons, flourishing with an abundance of produce. Being so colourful and varied in form, vegetables are great fun to use in embroidery, singly or in rows.

This border of carnation flowers is worked on evenweave fabric set into a guest towel. As it is a charted design, it would work equally well in needlepoint, as a cushion border for example.

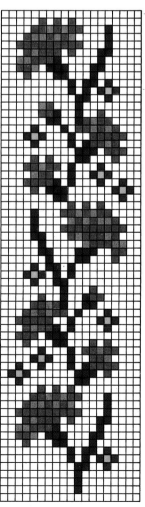

The country garden would not be complete without the delicate aroma of herbs. Use these motifs to create fresh designs for herb pillows or on a gardener's apron. In designing these motifs for the garden, it was impossible to ignore those little visitors – the caterpillars, butterflies and rabbits. Including them in your design work will add humour and a touch of realism. Embroider them on to everyday kitchen items like oven gloves and tea towels, or feature them on kitchen chair cushions.

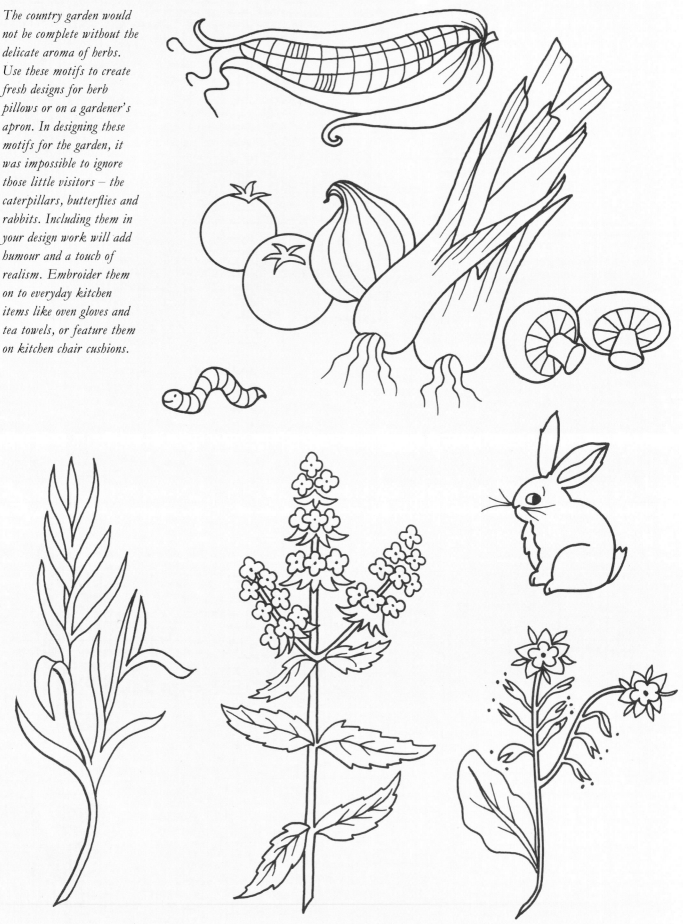

Presented here is a bevy of country maids for border, corner and panel designs. They are unashamedly romantic and I have found them a wonderful vehicle for exploring stitch patterns. Experiment with the shapes of the flowers and the design of the crinoline, applying real ribbons for a three-dimensional effect. For the spray of the watering can, follow the lines and add seed pearls.

Chapter 12

ANIMALS

There is something very special about meeting animals in their natural habitat and observing them feeding or at play. In the woods, in quiet country roads and at the sheltered edges of fields, it is often possible to get quite close to animal activity. Squirrels, rabbits, hedgehogs, pheasants and foxes are all fairly common sights on my country walks, badgers are more elusive, and as for solitary moles — well, I have yet to see one!

PREVIOUS PAGE This appealing hedgehog, a favourite countryside visitor, is set against a background of fields and flowers, hand stitched in a variety of threads.

ABOVE The brown and beige tones of the deer's dappled coat are echoed by the soft greens of the wild grasses. The vibrant red poppies add a splash of colour to this charming cross stitch panel.

RIGHT Inspired by the red squirrel, now nearly extinct in Britain, this needlepoint design shows the handsome animal surrounded by a display of leaves, berries and nuts for harvesting.

Animals were often portrayed on historical embroideries, especially animals of the chase like deer and wild boar. They were popular motifs on samplers, too, and I feel they must have provided the many young girls who stitched them with some light relief from lettering and numerals.

It is possible to build up exciting pieces of embroidery based on animal shapes, colours and textures, but also fun to explore the more humorous aspects of their characters. Children, especially, adore the whimsical appearance of some of our best-loved countryside animals.

Needlepoint and free-style embroidery are both suitable for animal motifs, which can be stitched realistically, perhaps with long-and-short stitch to represent their fur, or in a more stylized way. Their outlines are often simple enough to make successful quilting and appliqué designs, too.

This country cat looks very much at home among the wild flowers on a needlepoint pin cushion.

Countryside animals can be used in many ways in embroidery. They make good motifs for greetings cards or to personalize a gift, as so many people have a favourite animal which they would appreciate worked in stitchery.

As animals, especially baby ones, have such instant appeal for children, you can easily add little details to their clothes and accessories, perhaps playing up the design with clever position-ing. For example, the mole on page 128 would look just right emerging from a 'pocket' molehill, while the field mouse on his wheat stalk could follow the cable on a sweater.

For a more traditional result, a badger design would look very dramatic in blackwork on a white evenweave fabric, while a fox or otter could be worked in tent stitch for a needlepoint panel.

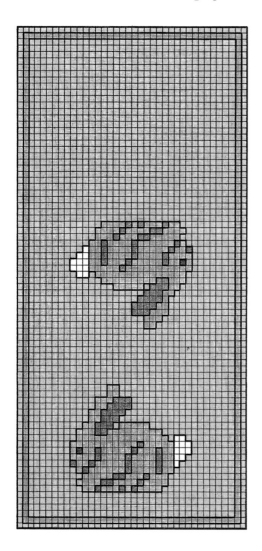

This tiny needlepoint purse features that countryside animal much-loved by all children – the rabbit. When the purse is folded, the rabbit appears on the back as well as the flap.

*This cross stitch cat is just
waiting to go on the prowl
in the fields and woods.
Mount the scene as a
special card or little
picture for a cat-lover.*

These cheerful animal motifs lend themselves to ideas for the nursery. A satin appliqué rabbit would look beautiful on a baby's sleeping bag, scattered with embroidered primrose sprigs. For an appealing picture, the sheep and lamb could be worked in woollen yarn on canvas or in French knots for texture on a thick fabric. The thirsty kittens are fun to add to a baby's bib and very quick to work, just in outline or filled in with satin stitch.

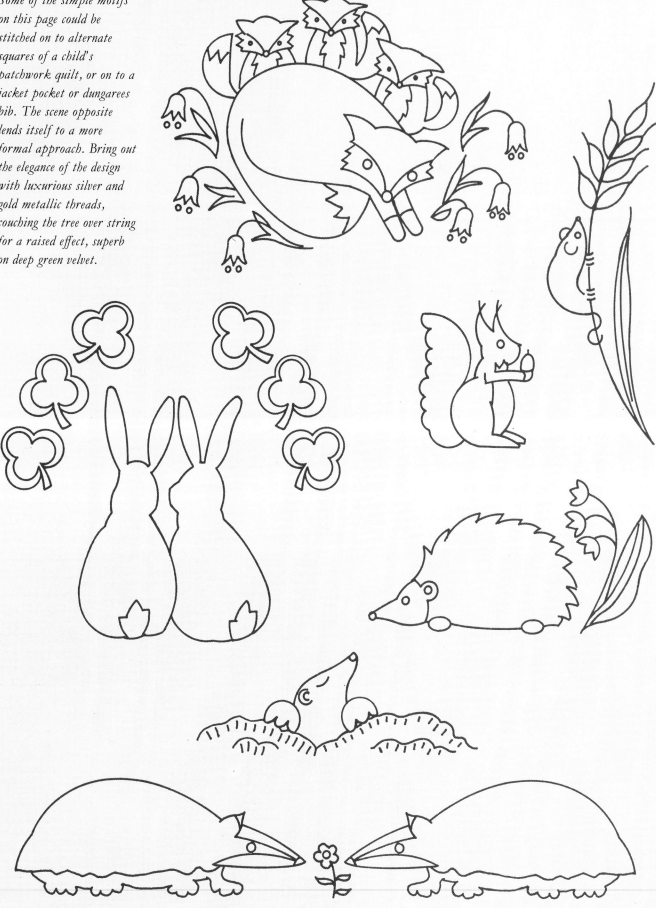

ANIMALS

Some of the simple motifs on this page could be stitched on to alternate squares of a child's patchwork quilt, or on to a jacket pocket or dungarees bib. The scene opposite lends itself to a more formal approach. Bring out the elegance of the design with luxurious silver and gold metallic threads, couching the tree over string for a raised effect, superb on deep green velvet.

MATERIALS, TECHNIQUES AND STITCHES

PLANNING YOUR EMBROIDERY.
Before you embark on any piece of embroidery, whether in free stitching, counted thread work, appliqué or quilting, take time to do some basic planning. Think about the feeling you are trying to create in your design and the use to which your work will be put. Then look at all the possible colours, fabrics and stitches you could use to achieve this.

This stage is always the most enjoyable for me: researching, planning alternatives and developing ideas before deciding on the final interpretation. My advice would be to follow your own instincts for each of your embroideries. In this way you will build on your own preferences and strengths, and gain in understanding with each piece of work you do.

The following guide-lines will help you with your planning and familiarize you with some of the materials, techniques and stitches you can use.

MATERIALS

THREADS There are many different types of embroidery thread in a huge range of colours, so do experiment with them instead of playing safe with just one or two familiar ones. Shiny threads include pearl cotton, coton à broder, pure silk and stranded cotton. The latter is very versatile as it can be split up into separate strands and recombined to make different thicknesses.

Different shades can be mixed in this way for subtle effects.

Soft embroidery cotton is a matt thread, slightly thicker than stranded cotton. There are also some beautiful metallic threads to add sparkle to your embroidery. Woollen yarns include tapestry wool, Persian wool and crewel wool, and textured knitting wool can often give interesting effects for a change.

FABRICS Free-style embroidery can be worked on all kinds of fabric, depending on the effect you want to achieve. Cotton and linen are ideal for garments or household items, providing an excellent base for embroidery. Silk is wonderful to work with and very luxurious. Oddments of dress or furnishing fabrics can make interesting backgrounds, and calico, being inexpensive, is useful for experimenting with different stitches.

For cross stitch work, you will need evenweave fabric with easily countable threads, while, for needlepoint, canvas is available in a range of mesh sizes.

NOTIONS You can make use of some of the notions available from haberdashery departments or craft shops to add interest to your embroidery. Beads, sequins, buttons, ribbons, lace, cord and braid can all be incorporated into a design to great effect, giving it texture and detail.

OPPOSITE Historical embroideries, like this example worked around 1720, are worth studying for their approach to colour and composition.

130

The life-like flowers and grasses in this panel detail are worked in a combination of machine and hand stitches on a painted background.

FABRIC PAINTS AND CRAYONS These add an extra dimension to an embroidery and are used by many designers to create subtle effects in their work. A painted fabric background can provide a coloured base for embroidery stitches which would be difficult to achieve in any other way.

There are paints and crayons available for use on both natural and synthetic fabrics. Depending on the type, these fabric colours can be applied with a brush, stencilled or sprayed on to fabric, or a design can be drawn on to paper and then transferred to the fabric by ironing.

EQUIPMENT

NEEDLES It is important to choose the correct type and size of needle for your work. Crewel needles have a long eye which will take various thicknesses of thread. Sharps are shorter with a smaller eye, suitable for only one or two strands of stranded cotton or for sewing thread. Betweens are short, sharp needles used in quilting. Tapestry needles are blunt and so do not split the threads of the fabric. They are used for needlepoint and cross stitch.

SCISSORS You will need a good pair of sharp pointed embroidery scissors for cutting threads and a pair of dressmaking shears for cutting fabric.

FRAMES Although some people prefer not to use a frame, it is important for many types of embroidery to work on stretched fabric. Both round and rectangular frames can be mounted on stands, leaving both hands free for stitching.

Ring frames are suitable for small areas of work and come in a range of diameters. It is a good idea to wrap a strip of thin fabric around the inner ring to protect the fabric on which you are working. Remember to remove your embroidery from the ring at the end of each work session, so as not to mark the fabric.

Mount larger pieces of work and needlepoint canvas on to a rectangular slate or rotating frame, or, alternatively, use artist's stretchers or even an old picture frame, attaching the fabric with drawing pins or staples.

TRACING THE DESIGN

Using a pencil, trace your chosen motifs from the book on to tracing paper. Then place the tracing paper on to a white background and sharpen up any lines which are not quite clear. Go over the entire design in black ink to give you good strong guide-lines.

At this stage, enlarge or reduce your motifs if you need to. You could do this by drawing a grid over your design and then copying it on to a larger or smaller grid. Alternatively, simply use a photocopier to enlarge or reduce it in size.

Also at this stage, you could digress into experimenting with colourways. Take advantage of technology again and make several photocopies of your design on which you can then try out colour ideas with felt tip pens or watercolours. If you have already decided on a colour scheme for your embroidery, match the thread colours on your photocopy to make sure they really do work together.

You can use your coloured copy to pin on to the background fabric to see the effectiveness of your idea, but remember to transfer the design from a clear black-and-white copy.

TRANSFERRING THE DESIGN TO FABRIC

There are several ways of transferring your design on to the fabric.

1. Place dressmaker's carbon paper face down on the fabric with your tracing on top. Then go over the lines with a sharp pencil. The carbon image will appear on the fabric.

2. Pin the tracing (or tissue) paper to the fabric and baste around all the lines with small stitches. Then score around the lines with a needle and pull the paper away to leave the tacked outline.

3. With a light fabric, tape your tracing to a clean white surface with the fabric over the top. Draw the lines, which will show through from the tracing, on to the fabric with a sharp hard crayon in an appropriate colour. If the tracing does not show through very clearly, it may help to tape it to a well-lit window instead.

You can use this method for transferring designs on to canvas, too, using an indelible marking pen. In this way, you can work the trace patterns in the book as needlepoint designs as well as in freestyle embroidery. You simply fill in the traced outlines with your chosen needlepoint stitches instead of having to follow a chart.

4. 'Prick and pounce' is a traditional method suitable for more intricate designs. With this method, you prick little holes all around the design outlines with a crewel needle. Then tape the tracing over the fabric on a board and, with a small felt pad, rub talc (for dark fabrics) or talc mixed with powdered charcoal (for light fabrics) through the holes. Join the dots with a fine line of watercolour paint.

USING A CHART

Needlepoint and cross stitch designs are usually worked by following a chart. Each square on the chart equals a needlepoint stitch or a cross stitch, which is worked on canvas or even-weave fabric.

Remember that the size of the mesh plays an important part in the size of the finished embroidery. A pattern worked on a 10-gauge canvas, for example, will be much bigger than the same pattern worked on 18-gauge canvas.

FINISHING OFF

If your embroidery needs pressing, place it face down on a thick towel or blanket covered with a clean white cloth. Cover the back of the embroidery with another cloth, then gently steam press from the back so that the stitches are not flattened.

Needlepoint may need to be stretched back into shape after it is finished. Dampen the needlepoint and place it face down on to several layers of blotting paper on a clean wooden board. Working from the centre outwards, stretch one edge at a time, pinning with rustproof drawing pins into the board. When the needlepoint is 'square', leave it to dry completely (which may take several days), then remove it from the board.

MOUNTING EMBROIDERY

If you would like to mount your work as a panel, a simple way is to stretch it over stiff card or hardboard. Make sure you leave a good border of fabric around your embroidery for turnings. Place the embroidery face down with the card, cut to the correct size, on top. Turn over the excess fabric and begin lacing from side to side with strong thread, starting at the centre of each side and working outwards each time. Repeat this process from top to bottom.

TECHNIQUES AND STITCHES

APPLIQUÉ Many of the designs in this book can be worked completely or partially in appliqué. Combining appliqué with embroidery will bring you some exciting effects, adding texture and areas of solid colour.

These needlepoint designs will have been worked by following a chart on which each square represents one stitch.

With fabrics that tend to fray, make a small turning all around the edge of the shape and stitch to the base fabric with slipstitch. Curves will need to be clipped first. Other, firmer fabrics can be attached with buttonhole or blanket stitch or, for speed, machine zigzag stitch.

QUILTING Motifs with a fairly simple outline can look very effective worked in quilting, and you can then use them to decorate padded items such as winter jackets or cot quilts. Padded quilting is worked through three layers of fabric – the top fabric, the wadding itself and the backing fabric. Synthetic wadding is available in a variety of thicknesses.

Once the motif is marked on to the top fabric, the layers need to be tacked firmly together, either in a grid formation or in lines radiating out from the centre. Then the design can be worked in small neat running stitches or alternatively in back stitch for a more pronounced outline.

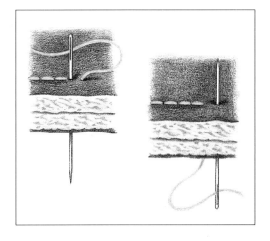

The padded effect in quilting is provided by a layer of wadding sandwiched between two layers of fabric. Running stitch or back stitch as shown here are used to outline the design.

USING WASTE CANVAS You may decide to work a cross stitch motif on to fabric which is too fine for the threads to be counted, for example, a flower sprig on a fine cotton blouse or a denim jacket. You can do this by working the stitches over 'waste' canvas which is made specially for this purpose. Tack it to the fabric, stitch the design and, when the motif is complete, dampen the embroidery so that the canvas threads can be withdrawn one by one, leaving the design on the fabric.

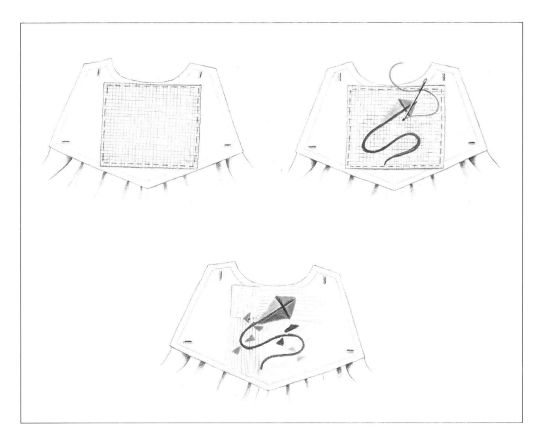

When using waste canvas, tack it to the fabric, work the cross stitch design over it and then withdraw the dampened canvas threads.

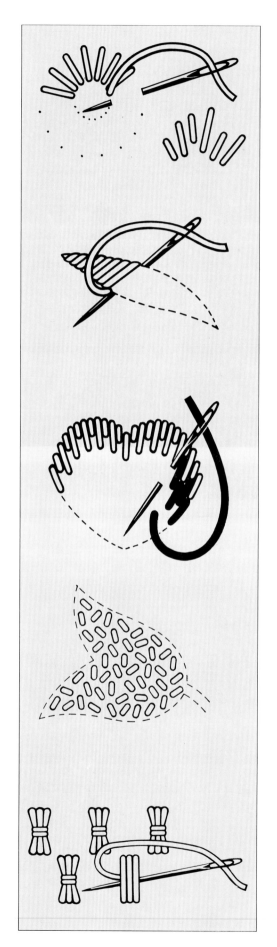

STITCH LIBRARY

FREE-STYLE STITCHES

STRAIGHT STITCH These are single stitches which can be worked in a regular fashion or just scattered at random. They can vary in length but should not be made too loose or long in case they snag.

SATIN STITCH This consists of straight stitches worked closely side by side across a shape. They can be upright or slanting, and may be padded slightly by working running stitch underneath. Satin stitch makes a beautiful smooth surface, and if shiny threads are used, reflects the light in an effective way.

LONG-AND-SHORT STITCH Beautiful shaded effects can be achieved with this stitch. It is very useful for filling shapes which are too big to be covered by satin stitch. Work the first row with alternate long and short stitches, following the outline of the shape. Fill in the following rows with stitches of similar lengths, keeping the embroidery smooth.

SEEDING This is a simple but useful filling stitch which gives a speckled effect. It is made up of short straight stitches scattered randomly over the fabric within a shape. For a varying density of tone, the stitches can be closely grouped in one area and spaced further apart in another.

SHEAF STITCH This filling stitch can be worked in staggered rows as shown or in horizontal rows with all the bundles of stitches in line with each other. Make three vertical satin stitches and tie them in the middle with two overcasting stitches. Then insert the needle into the fabric to move on to the next stitch group.

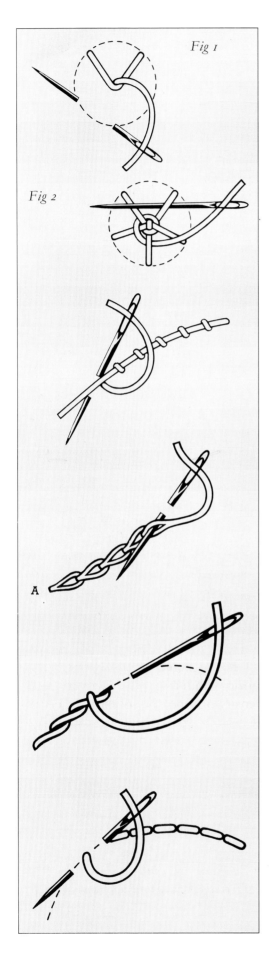

Fig 1

Fig 2

SPIDER'S WEB FILLING First make spokes around the circle as follows. Start with a fly stitch with a long tail, then work two straight stitches into the centre on either side of the tail (*fig. 1*). Weave the thread under and over the spokes to fill the circle (*fig. 2*).

COUCHING Lay a thread along the line of the motif. Then tie it down at regular intervals with another thread, using a contrasting colour or weight if required for effect.

SPLIT STITCH This is an outline stitch, but also works as a filling stitch where rows side by side make a fine flat surface. Bring the needle out at A, then take a small back stitch, piercing the thread with the needle tip as you pull it through.

STEM STITCH This is an ideal stitch for flower stems and outlines, but can also be arranged in rows side by side to fill in shapes. Working from left to right, make small even stitches along the outline, overlapping each stitch with the previous one as shown.

BACK STITCH A basic outline stitch, this can also be used in quilting instead of running stitch where a more defined line is required. Bring the needle through on the stitching line, take a small backward stitch and bring the needle out again a little further along. Take another backward stitch into the same hole as the previous stitch and so on.

CABLE STITCH Work cable stitch from left to right. Bring the needle through on the design line. Keeping thread below needle, insert the needle from right to left as in *fig. 1*. Work the next stitch in the same way, but this time keep the thread above the needle (*fig. 2*).

FRENCH KNOTS Bring the thread through and, holding it down with your left thumb, twist the needle around it twice as shown in *fig. 1*. Keeping the thread taut, insert the needle back into the fabric where it first came out, as shown by the arrow. Pull the thread through and bring to the front again for the next French knot (*fig. 2*).

BULLION KNOTS Make a back stitch the length you wish the bullion knot to be, bringing just the needle point back through at the beginning of the stitch. Twist the thread around the needle so that it equals the length of the back stitch. Keeping the thread taut, pull the needle through and take it back to the beginning of the stitch (see arrow).

CORAL STITCH The knots in coral stitch can be spaced closely or further apart. Start at the right of the design. Lay the thread along the line, holding it down with your thumb. Make a tiny stitch under the line and, with thread under needle, draw through and pull up gently to form a knot.

BLANKET STITCH Blanket stitch (or buttonhole stitch if closed up) is useful for working around appliqué shapes. Bring the thread through on the lower line, make a stitch from the upper to the lower line and, with the thread under the needle, pull the stitch through.

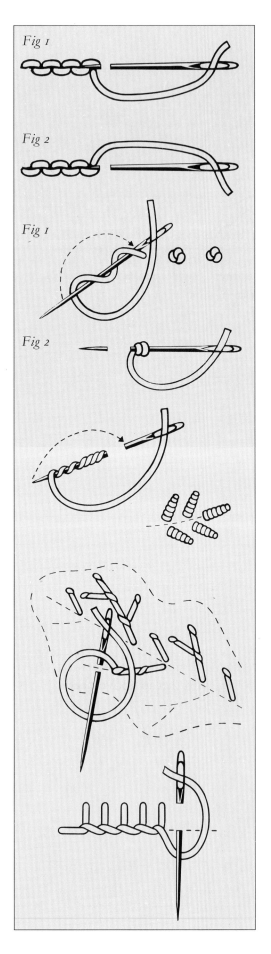

Fig 1

Fig 2

Fig 1

Fig 2

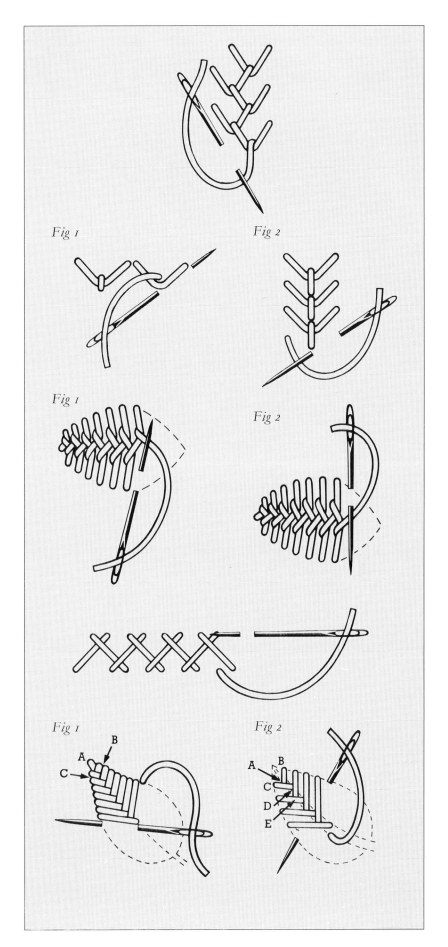

FEATHER STITCH Bring the thread through at the top centre. Insert the needle to the right and make a stitch downwards towards the centre, keeping the thread under the needle. Next, insert the needle to the left and make another stitch downwards and towards the centre with the thread under the needle.

FLY STITCH Fly stitch may be worked in horizontal rows (*fig. 1*) or vertical rows (*fig. 2*), or alternatively as single stitches. Bring the needle through at top left and insert it again to the right, holding the thread down with your thumb. Make a small tying stitch to anchor the loop, as shown.

CRETAN STITCH Start centrally on the left of the shape. Take a small stitch from the lower line towards the centre with thread under needle (*fig. 1*). Then take a stitch from the upper line in the same way, with thread under needle (*fig. 2*).

HERRINGBONE STITCH Bring the thread through at the bottom. Moving slightly to the right, insert the needle from right to left along the top line and pull through, with thread below needle. Again moving to the right, make another stitch from right to left, with thread above needle.

FISHBONE STITCH *Fig. 1* shows the closed version of the stitch. Make a small stitch from A along the centre line of the motif. Bring the thread out at B and make a slanting stitch across the base of the first stitch. Come out at C, then make another slanting stitch across the base of the previous stitch and so on. *Fig. 2* shows the open version of the stitch. Bring the thread out at A and follow in sequence.

Fig 1   *Fig 2*

Fig 1   *Fig 2*

Fig 1   *Fig 2*

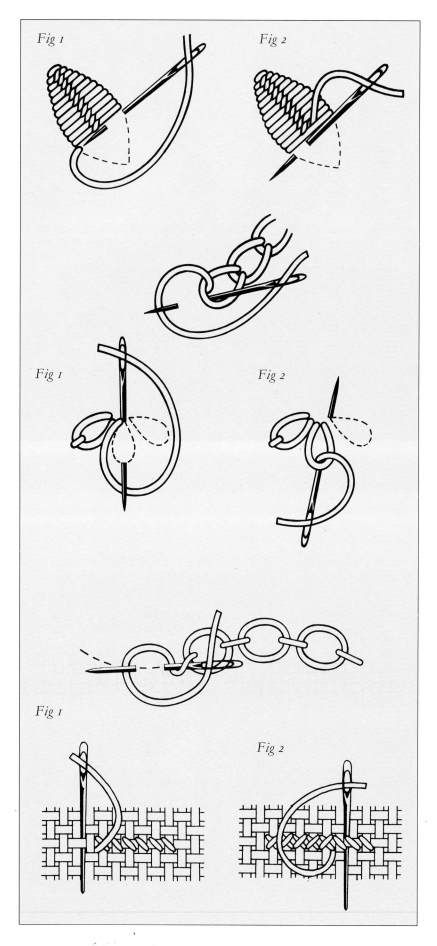

Fig 1   Fig 2

Fig 1   Fig 2

Fig 1

Fig 2

ROUMANIAN STITCH Bring the thread out at the left of the motif, take it to the right and make a stitch to the centre with thread below needle (*fig. 1*). Take another stitch from centre to left with the thread above the needle (*fig. 2*). This makes a small tying stitch as shown.

CHAIN STITCH Chain stitch can be used as a filling stitch if worked in adjacent rows or as a spiral. It is also an outline stitch. Bring the thread through at the top of the line. Reinsert the needle in the same place and, holding down the loop with your thumb, bring the needle out a short way down. Pull the thread through to form a chain.

DETACHED CHAIN STITCH This is worked in the same way as chain stitch (*fig. 1*), but each loop is anchored down with a small stitch (*fig. 2*). The stitches can be worked singly, grouped into flower petals or scattered over the fabric like seeding.

CABLE CHAIN STITCH Bring the needle through at right. Holding the thread down with your left thumb, twist the needle round the thread as shown. Make a loop, hold it down with your thumb and take a stitch with thread under needle. This makes alternate chain stitches and linking stitches.

COUNTED THREAD

CROSS STITCH The crosses are worked in two stages. First work a row of half cross stitch from right to left (*fig. 1*), then work back the other way to complete the crosses (*fig. 2*). The top arm of each cross stitch should slope in the same direction.

NEEDLEPOINT STITCHES

TENT STITCH Tent stitch can be worked either in diagonal rows as in *figs. 1 and 2* or in horizontal rows as in *figs. 3 and 4*. The former method is preferable, where possible, as it prevents the canvas from being distorted by the stitching.

HALF CROSS STITCH This needlepoint stitch resembles tent stitch but is worked differently. It is useful when embroidering with a thick yarn, as it is not as bulky. Each diagonal stitch is worked over one canvas intersection and the stitches on the back are vertical.

BRICK STITCH This consists of vertical stitches worked in staggered rows. In *fig. 1* long and short stitches are worked alternately. In *fig. 2*, the next and all subsequent rows interlock neatly with the one above.

HUNGARIAN STITCH This consists of interlocking rows of a small diamond pattern and is very effective worked in more than one colour. The vertical straight stitches are worked in groups over two, four and two canvas threads respectively, leaving two canvas threads between each group. Each row fits into the previous one.

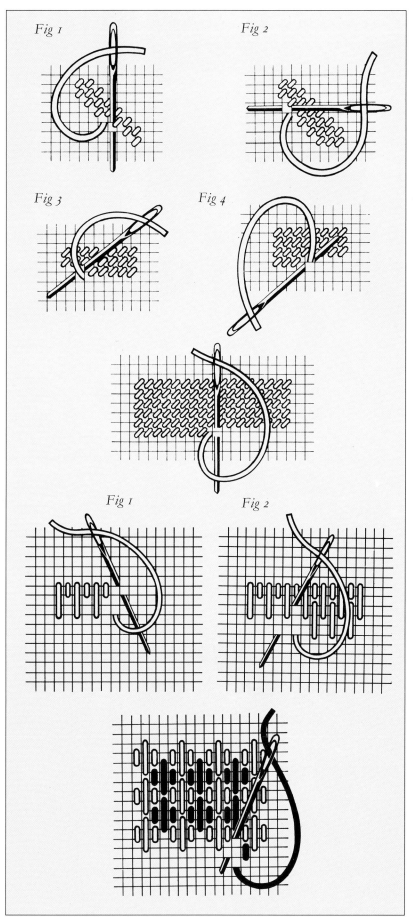

Fig 1   Fig 2

Fig 3   Fig 4

Fig 1   Fig 2

INDEX

The page numbers in *italics* refer to the illustrations.

ACKNOWLEDGMENTS

The publishers would like to thank the following embroidery designers for kindly allowing their work to be reproduced in this book:

Jacket embroidery Marina Williams
5 Gillian Wall
7 Members of the Kingston Branch of the Embroiderers' Guild
8–9 Mary Hickmott
20–1 Bette Uscott-Woolsey
22 Alan and Carol Phillipson Designs/Wrencraft Needlework Kits
26–7 Wilma Shields and Katrina Witten/Rowandean Embroidery Kits
38–9 Sandara Hurll
40 (top) Gillian Wall
41 Barbara Fray/Networks

42 Gail Lawther
48–9 Caroline Palmer
50 Annette Woollard/Applegate Designs
51 Gail Lawther
53 Gail Lawther
60–1 Annette Woollard/Applegate Designs
68–9 Judy Hares
70 Ljiljana Rylands
71 Wilma Shields and Katrina Witten/Rowandean Embroidery Kits
78–9 Barbara Fray/Networks
80 (top) Gillian Wall
90–1 Gillian Wall
94 Gail Lawther
100–1 Rosemary Jarvis
102 (top) Moyra McNeill
102 (bottom) Rosemary Jarvis

103 Moyra McNeill
104 (top) Ann V. Sutton
110–11 Sara Norrish
112 Gail Lawther
120–21 Wilma Shields and Katrina Witten/Rowandean Embroidery Kits
122 (top) Alan and Carol Phillipson Designs/Wrencraft Needlework Kits
122 (bottom) Stella Edwards
132 Evelyn Jennings

The photographs on the following pages are reproduced with the permission of:

11, 104, 113, 123 Tracey Orme
131 e.t. archives/Victoria and Albert Museum, London

⚓ Anchor

Coats Crafts internationally market a comprehensive and diverse range of handicraft threads and accessories. The trade mark Anchor represents a wide choice of top quality products for all types of embroidery, tapestry and crochet.
Details of Anchor suppliers are available from:

UNITED KINGDOM

Coats Patons Crafts
PO Box, McMullen Road
Darlington
Co. Durham DL1 1YQ
Tel: (0325) 381010
Fax: (0325) 382300

USA

Coats and Clark
PO Box 24998
30 Patewood Drive
Suite 351
Greenville SC 29615
Tel: (803) 234-0331
Fax: (803) 675-5609

CANADA

Coats Patons
1001 Roselawn Ave
Toronto
Ontario M6B 1B8
Tel: (416) 782-4481
Fax: (416) 785-1370

AUSTRALIA

Coats Patons Crafts
89–91 Peters Ave
Mulgrave
Victoria 3170
Tel: (03) 561-2288
Fax: (03) 561-2298

NEW ZEALAND

Coats Patons (New Zealand) Ltd
263 Ti Rakau Drive
Pakuranga
Auckland
Tel: (09) 274-0021
Fax: (09) 274-7228

SOUTH AFRICA

Coats Tootal
PO Box 347
Randfontein 1760
Tel: (011) 693-5130
Fax: (011) 692-3957